STRENGTHEN
yourself in
THE LORD
LEADER'S GUIDE

DESTINY IMAGE BOOKS BY BILL JOHNSON

STRENGTHEN
yourself in
THE LORD
LEADER'S GUIDE

How to Release the Hidden Power of God
In Your Life

BILL JOHNSON

Leader's Guide prepared by Larry Sparks

DESTINY IMAGE® PUBLISHERS, INC.
P.O. Box 310, Shippensburg, PA 17257-0310
"Promoting Inspired Lives."

This book and all other Destiny Image and Destiny Image Fiction books are available at Christian bookstores and distributors worldwide.

Cover design by Eileen Rockwell

For more information on foreign distributors, call 717-532-3040.

Reach us on the Internet: www.destinyimage.com.

ISBN 13 TP: 978-0-7684-0778-5

For Worldwide Distribution, Printed in the U.S.A.
1 2 3 4 5 6 7 8 / 19 18 17 16 15

CONTENTS

BASIC LEADER GUIDELINES

This study is designed to help you develop into a believer who can go through any difficult situation and maintain a supernatural attitude and perspective. From *this* perspective, you will partner with God to see impossibilities bow at Jesus' name and step into the destiny God has for you!

There are several different ways that you can engage this study. By no means is this forthcoming list comprehensive. Rather, these are the standard outlets recommended to facilitate this curriculum. We encourage you to seek the Lord's direction, be creative, and prepare for supernatural transformation in your Christian life.

When all is said and done, this curriculum is unique in that the end goal is *not* information—it is transformation. The sessions are intentionally sequenced to take every believer on a journey from information, to revelation, to transformation. Participants will receive a greater understanding of what partnership with Heaven looks like and learn how to practically live this supernatural lifestyle on a daily basis.

Here are some of the ways you can use the curriculum:

1. Church Small Group

Often, churches feature a variety of different small group opportunities per season in terms of books, curriculum resources, and Bible studies. *Strengthen Yourself in the Lord* would be included among the offering of titles for whatever season you are launching for the small group program.

It is recommended that you have at least four to five people to make up a small group and a maximum of twelve. If you end up with more than 12 members, either the group needs to multiply and break into two different groups or you should consider moving toward a church class model (which will be outlined below).

For a small group setting, here are the essentials:

- *Meeting place*: Either the leader's home or a space provided by the church.

- *Appropriate technology*: A DVD player attached to a TV that is large enough for all of the group members to see (and loud enough for everyone to hear).

- *Leader/Facilitator*: This person will often be the host, if the small group is being conducted at someone's home; but it can also be a team (husband/wife, two church leaders, etc.). The leader(s) will direct the session from beginning to end, from sending reminder e-mails to participating group members about the meetings, to closing out the sessions in prayer and dismissing everyone. That said, leaders might select certain people in the group to assist with various elements of the meeting—worship, prayer, ministry time, etc. A detailed description of what the group meetings should look like will follow in the pages to come.

Sample Schedule for Home Group Meeting (for a 7:00 P.M. Meeting)

- Before arrival: Ensure that refreshments are ready by 6:15 P.M. If they need to be refrigerated, ensure they are preserved appropriately until 15 minutes prior to the official meeting time.

- 6:15 P.M.: Leaders arrive at meeting home or facility.

- 6:15–6:25 P.M.: Connect with hosts, co-hosts, and/or co-leaders to review the evening's program.

- 6:25–6:35 P.M.: Pray with hosts, co-hosts, and/or co-leaders for the evening's events. Here are some sample prayer directives:
  - For the Holy Spirit to move and minister freely.
  - For the teaching to connect with and transform all who hear it.

- For dialogue and conversation that edifies.
- For comfort and transparency among group members.
- For the Presence of God to manifest during worship.
- For testimonies of answered prayers.
- For increased hunger for God's Presence and power.

- 6:35–6:45: Ensure technology is functioning properly!
  - Test the DVDs featuring the teaching sessions, making sure they are set up to the appropriate session.
  - If you are doing praise and worship, ensure that either the MP3 player or CD player is functional, set at an appropriate volume (not soft, but not incredibly loud), and that song sheets are available for everyone so they can sing along with the lyrics. (If you are tech savvy, you could do a PowerPoint or Keynote presentation featuring the lyrics.)

- 6:45–7:00 P.M.: Welcome and greeting for guests.

- 7:00–7:10 P.M.: Fellowship, community, and refreshments.

- 7:10–7:12 P.M.: Gather everyone together in the meeting place.

- 7:12–7:30 P.M.: Introductory prayer and worship.

- 7:30–7:40 P.M.: Ministry and prayer time.

- 7:40–8:00 P.M.: Watch DVD session.

- 8:00–8:20 P.M.: Discuss DVD session.

- 8:20–8:35 P.M.: Activation time.

- 8:35–8:40 P.M.: Closing prayer and dismiss.

This sample scheduled is *not* intended to lock you into a formula. It is simply provided as a template to help you get started. Our hope is that you customize it according to the unique needs of your group and sensitively navigate the activity of the Holy Spirit as He uses these sessions to supernaturally transform the lives of every person participating in the study.

2. SMALL GROUP CHURCH-WIDE CAMPAIGN

This would be the decision of the pastor or senior leadership of the church. In this model, the entire church would go through *Strengthen Yourself in the Lord* in both the main services and ancillary small groups/ life classes.

These campaigns would be marketed as *40 Days of Strength* or *40 Days to Strengthen Yourself in the Lord.* The pastor's weekend sermon would be based on the principles in *Strengthen Yourself in the Lord,* and the Sunday school classes/life classes and/or small groups would also follow the *Strengthen Yourself in the Lord* curriculum format.

3. CHURCH CLASS | MID-WEEK CLASS | SUNDAY SCHOOL CURRICULUM

Churches of all sizes offer a variety of classes purposed to develop members into more effective disciples of Jesus and agents of transformation in their spheres of influence.

Strengthen Yourself in the Lord would be an invaluable addition to a church's class offering. Typically, churches offer a variety of topical classes targeted at men's needs, women's needs, marriage, family, finances, and various areas of Bible study.

Strengthen Yourself in the Lord is a unique resource, as it does not fit in with the aforementioned traditional topics usually offered to the Church body. On the contrary, this study breaks down what it means to strengthen your inner self in the Lord, and shows believers how to start living victoriously from Heaven's perspective and supernaturally transform the world around them.

While it may difficult to facilitate dialogue in a class setting, it is certainly optional and recommended. The other way to successfully engage *Strengthen Yourself in the Lord* in a class setting is to have a teacher/leader go through the questions/answers presented in the upcoming pages and use these as his or her teaching notes.

4. INDIVIDUAL STUDY

While the curriculum is designed for use in a group setting, it also works as a tool that can equip anyone who is looking to strengthen his or her spirit and soul.

STEPS TO LAUNCHING A *STRENGTHEN YOURSELF IN THE LORD* GROUP OR CLASS

PREPARE WITH PRAYER!

Pray! If you are a **church leader**, prayerfully consider how *Strengthen Yourself in the Lord* could transform the culture and climate of your church community! The Lord is raising up bodies of believers who bring transformation in their wake because of the overflow of a mind that's been reoriented to Heaven's perspective. Spend some time with the Holy Spirit, asking Him to give you vision for what this unique study will do for your church, and, ultimately, how a Kingdom-minded people will transform your city and region.

If you are a **group leader** or **class facilitator**, pray for those who will be attending your group, signing up for your class, and will be positioning their lives to be transformed by the Power and Presence of God in this study.

PREPARE PRACTICALLY!

Determine how you will be using the Strengthen Yourself in the Lord curriculum.

Identify which of the following formats you will be using the curriculum in:

- Church-sponsored small group study

- Church-wide campaign

- Church class (Wednesday night, Sunday morning, etc.)

- Individual study

Determine a meeting location and ensure availability of appropriate equipment.

Keep in mind the number of people who may attend. You will also need AV (audio-visual) equipment. The more comfortable the setting, the more people will enjoy being there, and will spend more time ministering to each other!

A word of caution here: the larger the group, the greater the need for co-leaders or assistants. The ideal small group size is difficult to judge; however, once you get more than 10 to 12 people, it becomes difficult for each member to feel "heard." If your group is larger than 12 people, consider either having two or more small group discussion leaders or "multiplying" the larger group into two smaller ones.

Determine the format for your meetings.

The Presence of the Lord, which brings transformation, is cradled and stewarded well in the midst of organization. Structure should never replace spontaneity; on the contrary, having a plan and determining what type of format your meetings will take enables you to flow with the Holy Spirit and minister more effectively.

Also, by determining what kind of meeting you will be hosting, you become well equipped to develop a schedule for the meeting, identify potential co-leaders, and order the appropriate number of resources.

Set a schedule for your meetings.

Once you have established the format for your meetings, set a schedule for your meetings. Some groups like to have a time of fellowship or socializing (either before or after the meeting begins) where light refreshments are offered. Some groups will want to incorporate times of worship and personal ministry into the small group or class. This is highly recommended for *Strengthen Yourself in the Lord,* as the study is designed to be founded upon equipping and activating believers through encountering God's Presence. The video portion and discussion questions are intended to instruct believers, while the worship, times of ministry, group interaction, prayer time, and activation elements are purposed to engage them to live out what they just learned. *Strengthen Yourself in the Lord* is not a lofty theological concept; it is a practical reality for every born-again believer. This study is intended to educate; but even more so, it is designed to activate believers and position them to steward their private, interior lives.

Establish a start date along with a weekly meeting day and time.
This eight-week curriculum should be followed consistently and consecutively. Be mindful of the fact that while there are eight weeks of material, most groups will want to meet one last time after completing the last week to celebrate, or designate their first meeting as a time to get to know each other and "break the ice." This is very normal and should be encouraged to continue the community momentum that the small group experience initiates. Typically, after the final session is completed, groups will often engage in a social activity—either going out to dinner together, seeing a movie, or something of the like.

Look far enough ahead on the calendar to account for anything that might interfere. Choose a day that works well for the members of your group. For a church class, be sure to coordinate the time with the appropriate ministry leader.

Advertise!
Getting the word out in multiple ways is most effective. Print out flyers, post a sign-up sheet, make an announcement in church services or group meetings, send out weekly e-mails and text messages, set up your own blog or website, or post the event on the social media avenue you and your group utilize most (Facebook, Twitter, etc.). A personal invitation or phone call is a great way

to reach those who might need that little bit of extra encouragement to get involved.

For any type of small group or class to succeed, it must be endorsed by and encouraged from the leadership. For larger churches with multiple group/class offerings, it is wise to provide church members literature featuring all of the different small group/class options. This information should also be displayed online in an easily accessible page on your church website.

For smaller churches, it is a good idea for the pastor or a key leader to announce the launch of a small group course or class from the pulpit during an announcement time.

Gather your materials.

Each leader will need the *Strengthen Yourself in the Lord Leader's Kit,* as well as the *Strengthen Yourself in the Lord* book.

Additionally, each participant will need a personal copy of the *Strengthen Yourself in the Lord* workbook. It is recommended they also purchase the *Strengthen Yourself in the Lord* book for further enrichment and as a resource to complement their daily readings. However, they are able to engage in the exercises and participate in the group discussion apart from reading the book.

We have found it best for the materials to all be purchased at one time—many booksellers and distributors offer discounts on multiple orders, and you are assured that each member will have their materials from the beginning of the course.

Step Forward!

Arrive at your meeting in *plenty* of time to prepare; frazzled last-minute preparations do not put you in a place of "rest," and your group members will sense your stress! Ensure that all AV equipment is working properly and that you have ample supplies for each member. Name tags are a great idea, at least for the first couple of meetings. Icebreaker and introduction activities are also a good idea for the first meeting.

Pray for your members. As much as possible, make yourself available to them. As members increase in insight on strengthening themselves in the Lord, they will want to share that discovery! You will also need to encourage those who struggle, grow weary, or lose heart along the journey and through the process. Make sure your members stay committed so they experience the full benefits of this teaching.

Embrace the journey that you and your fellow members are embarking on to strengthen themselves in the Lord. Transformation begins within *you*!

Multiply yourself. Is there someone you know who was not able to attend your group? Help them to initiate their own small group now that you know how effective hosting *Strengthen Yourself in the Lord* can be in a group setting!

Thank You

Thank you for embarking on a journey to equip the bride of Christ to be strong, peaceful, joyful, and who she is destined to be in this world.

LEADER CHECKLIST

ONE TO TWO MONTHS PRIOR

_____ Have you determined a start date for your class or small group?

_____ Have you determined the format, meeting day and time, and weekly meeting schedule?

_____ Have you selected a meeting location (making sure you have adequate space and AV equipment available)?

_____ Have you advertised? Do you have a sign-up sheet to ensure you order enough materials?

THREE WEEKS TO ONE MONTH PRIOR

_____ Have you ordered materials? You will need a copy of *Strengthen Yourself in the Lord* Curriculum Kit, along with copies of the workbook and book for each participant.

_____ Have you organized your meeting schedule/format?

ONE TO TWO WEEKS PRIOR

_____ Have you received all your materials?

_____ Have you reviewed the DVDs and your Leader's Kit to familiarize yourself with the material and to ensure everything is in order?

_____ Have you planned and organized the refreshments, if you are planning to provide them? Some leaders will handle this themselves, and some find it easier to allow participants to sign up to provide refreshments if they would like to do so.

_____ Have you advertised and promoted? This includes sending out emails to all participants, setting up a Facebook group, setting up a group through your church's database system (if available), promotion in the church bulletin, etc.

_____ Have you appointed co-leaders to assist you with the various portions of the group/class? While it is not necessary, it is helpful to have someone who is in charge of either leading (on guitar, keyboard, etc.) or arranging the worship music (putting songs on a CD, creating song lyric sheets, etc.). It is also helpful to have a prayer coordinator as well—someone who helps facilitate the prayer time, ensuring that all of the prayer needs are acknowledged and remembered, and assigning the various requests to group members who are willing to lift up those needs in prayer.

FIRST MEETING DAY

_____ Plan to arrive *early!* Give yourself extra time to set up the meeting space, double check all AV equipment, and organize your materials. It might be helpful to ask participants to arrive 15 minutes early for the first meeting to allow for distribution of materials and any icebreaker activity you might have planned.

Session Discussion Questions

WEEKLY OVERVIEW OF
MEETINGS/GROUP SESSIONS

Here are some instructions on how to use each of the weekly Discussion Question guides.

WELCOME AND FELLOWSHIP
TIME (10–15 MINUTES)

This usually begins five to ten minutes prior to the designated meeting time and typically continues up until ten minutes after the official starting time. Community is important. One of the issues in many small group/class environments is the lack of connectivity among the people. People walk around inspired and resourced, but they remain disconnected from other believers. Foster an environment where community is developed but, at the same time, not distracting. Distraction tends to be a problem that plagues small group settings more than classes.

Welcome: Greet everyone as they walk in. If it is a small group environment, as the host or leader, be intentional about connecting with each person as they enter the meeting space. If it is a church class environment, it is still recommended that the leader connect with each participant. However, there will be less pressure for the participants to feel connected immediately in a traditional class setting versus a more intimate small group environment.

Refreshments and materials: In the small group, you can serve refreshments and facilitate fellowship between group members. In a class setting, talk with the attendees and ensure that they purchase all of their necessary materials (workbook and optional copy of *Strengthen Yourself in the Lord*). Ideally, the small group members will have received all of their resources prior to Week 1, but if not, ensure that the materials are present at the meeting and available for group members to pick up or purchase. It is advisable that you have several copies of the workbook and book available at the small group meeting, just in case people did not receive their copies at the designated time.

Call the meeting to order: This involves gathering everyone together in the appropriate place and clearly announcing that the meeting is getting ready to start.

Pray! Open every session in prayer, specifically addressing the topic that you will be covering in the upcoming meeting time. Invite the Presence of the Holy Spirit to come, move among the group members, minister to them individually, reveal Jesus, and stir greater hunger in each participant to experience *more* of God's power in their lives.

INTRODUCTIONS (10 MINUTES— FIRST CLASS ONLY)

While a time of formal introduction should only be done on the first week of the class/session, it is recommended that in subsequent meetings group members state their names when addressing a question, making a prayer request, giving a comment, etc., just to ensure everyone is familiar with names. You are also welcome to do a short icebreaker activity at this time.

Introduce yourself and allow each participant to briefly introduce him/herself. This should work fine for both small group and class environments. In a small group, you can go around the room and have each person introduce himself/herself one at a time. In a classroom setting, establish some type of flow and then have each person give a quick introduction (name, interesting factoid, etc.).

Discuss the schedule for the meetings. Provide participants an overview of what the next eight weeks will look like. If you plan to do any type of social activities, you might want to advertise this right up front, noting that while the curriculum runs for eight weeks, there will be a ninth session dedicated to fellowship and some type of fun activity.

Distribute materials to each participant. Briefly orient the participants to the book and workbook, explaining the 10–15 minute time commitment for every day (Monday through Friday). Encourage each person to engage fully in this journey—they will get out of it only

as much as they invest. The purpose for the daily reinforcement activities is *not* to add busy work to their lives.
This is actually a way to cultivate a habit of Bible study
and daily time renewing their minds, starting with just
10–15 minutes a day. Morning, evening, afternoon—
when does not matter. The key is making the decision
to engage.

WORSHIP (15 MINUTES—OPTIONAL FOR THE FIRST MEETING)

Fifteen minutes is a solid time for a worship segment.
That said, it all depends upon the culture of your group.
If everyone is okay with doing 30 minutes of praise and
worship, by all means, go for it!

For this particular curriculum, a worship segment is
highly recommended, as true and lasting transformation
happens as we continually encounter God's presence.

If a group chooses to do a worship segment, usually
they decide to begin on the second week. It often
takes an introductory meeting for everyone to become
acquainted with one another, and comfortable with
their surroundings before they open up together in
worship.

On the other hand, if the group members are already
comfortable with one another and they are ready to
launch immediately into a time of worship, they should
definitely begin on the first meeting.

While it has been unusual for Sunday school/church
classes to have a time of worship during their sessions,

it is actually a powerful way to prepare participants to receive the truth being shared in the *Strengthen Yourself in the Lord* sessions. In addition, pre-service worship (if the class is being held prior to a Sunday morning worship experience) actually stirs hunger in the participants for greater encounters with God's presence, both corporately and congregationally.

If the class is held mid-week (or on a day where there is *no* church service going on), a praise and worship component is a wonderful way to refresh believers in God's Presence as they are given the privilege of coming together, mid-week, and corporately experiencing His Presence.

PRAYER/MINISTRY TIME (5–15 MINUTES)

At this point, you will transition from either welcome or worship into a time of prayer.

Just like praise and worship, it is recommended that this initial time of prayer be five to ten minutes in length; but if the group is made up of people who do not mind praying longer, it should not be discouraged. The key is stewarding everyone's time well while maintaining focus on the most important things at hand.

Prayer should be navigated carefully, as there will always be people who use it as an opportunity to speak longer than necessary, vent about the circumstances in their lives, or potentially gossip about other people.

At the same time, there are real people carrying deep needs to the group and they need supernatural ministry.

The prayer component is a time where group members will not just receive prayer, but also learn how to exercise Jesus' authority in their own lives and witness breakthrough in their circumstances.

This prayer time doubles as a ministry time, where believers are encouraged to flow in the gifts of the Holy Spirit. After the door is opened through worship, the atmosphere is typically charged with God's Presence. It is quite common for people to receive words of knowledge, words of wisdom, prophetic words, and for other manifestations of the Holy Spirit to take place in these times (see 1 Cor. 12). This is a safe environment for people to "practice" these gifts, take risks, etc. However, if there are individuals who demonstrate consistent disorder, are unceasingly distracting, have problems/issues that move beyond the scope of this particular curriculum (and appear to need specialized counseling), or have issues that veer more into the theological realm, it is best for you to refer these individuals to an appropriate leader in the church who can address these particular issues privately.

If you are such a leader, you can either point them to a different person, or you can encourage them to save their questions/comments and you will address them outside of the group context, as you do not want to distract from what God is doing in these vital moments together.

TRANSITION TIME

At this point, you will transition from prayer/ministry time to watching the *Strengthen Yourself in the Lord* DVDs.

Group leaders/class teachers: It is recommended that you have the DVD in the player and are all ready to press "play" on the appropriate session.

VIDEO/TEACHING (20–25 MINUTES)

During this time, group members will fill in the blanks in their participant workbooks. All of the information they need to complete this assignment will appear on screen during the session. However, there will be additional information that appears on screen that will *not* go in the "fill in the blank" section. This is simply for the viewer's own notation.

SCRIPTURE

We have selected a Scripture passage that accompanies the theme for the week. You or someone else can read this out loud.

SUMMARY

There is also short summary of the week's topic before the discussion questions. You can read this prior to the group meeting to provide you with a summary of that week's session.

DISCUSSION QUESTIONS (20–30 MINUTES)

In the Leader's Guide there will be a number of questions to ask the group, most of which are in the workbook also. Some questions will be phrased so you can ask them directly, others may have instructions or suggestions for how you can guide the discussion. The sentences in bold are directions for you.

Some lessons will have more questions than others. Also, there might be some instances where you choose to cut out certain questions for the sake of time. This is entirely up to you, and in a circumstance where the Holy Spirit is moving and appears to be highlighting some questions more than others, flow in sync with the Holy Spirit. He will not steer you wrong!

Some of the questions will lead with a Scripture verse. To engage group members, you can ask for volunteers to read the Scripture verse(s). As you ask the question in the group setting, encourage more than one person to provide an answer. Usually, you will have some people who are way off in their responses, but you will also have those who provide *part* of the correct answer.

The problem with many curriculum studies is in the question/answer section. Participants may feel like the conversation was lively, the dialogue insightful, and that the meeting was an overall success; but when all is said and done, the question, *"What do I do next?"* is not sufficiently answered.

This is why every discussion time will be followed with an activation segment.

ACTIVATION (5–25 MINUTES)

- Each activation segment should be five to ten minutes at the *minimum*, as this is the place where believers begin putting action to what they just learned.

- The activation segment will be tailored to the session covered.

- Even though every group member might not be able to participate in the activation exercise, it gives them a visual for what it looks like to demonstrate the concept that they just studied.

PLANS FOR THE NEXT WEEK (2 MINUTES)

Remind group members about daily exercises in the workbook. Encourage everyone to participate fully in this journey in order to get the most out of it. The daily exercises should not take more than 15–20 minutes and they will make an ideal 40-day themed Bible study.

Be sure to let group members know if the meeting location will change or differ from week to week, or if there are any other relevant announcements to your group/class. Weekly e-mails, Facebook updates, and text messages are great tools to communicate with your group. If your church has a database tool that allows for communication between small group/class leaders and members, that is an effective avenue for interaction as well.

CLOSE IN PRAYER

This is a good opportunity to ask for a volunteer to conclude the meeting with prayer.

Week 1

Preparing for Your Promotion

Prayer Focus: Ask the Lord to help every participant 1) understand the importance of the preparation seasons that come before promotion, and 2) learn how to strengthen themselves in the Lord during those times.

Fellowship, Welcome, and Introductions
(20-30 MINUTES—FOR THE FIRST MEETING)

Welcome everyone as they walk in. If it is a small group environment, as the host or leader, be intentional about connecting with each person as they come to the meeting space. If it is a church class environment, it is still recommended that the leader connects with each participant. However, there will be less pressure for the participants to feel connected immediately in a traditional class setting versus a more intimate small group environment.

In the small group, serve refreshments and facilitate fellowship between group members. In a class setting, talk with the attendees and ensure that they receive all of their necessary materials (the workbook and a copy of *Strengthen Yourself in the Lord*).

Introduce yourself and allow participants to briefly introduce themselves as well. This should work fine for both small group and class environments. In a small group, you can go around the room and have each person introduce him or herself, one at a time. In a classroom setting, establish some type of flow and then have each person give a quick introduction (name, interesting factoid, etc.).

Discuss the schedule for the meetings. Provide participants an overview of what the next eight weeks will look like. If you plan to do any type of social activities, you might want to advertise this at the start, noting that while the curriculum runs for eight weeks, there will be a ninth meeting dedicated to fellowship and some type of fun activity. However, you might come up with this idea later on in the actual study.

Distribute materials to each participant. Briefly orient the participants to the book and workbook, explaining the 15–20 minute time commitment for each day. Encourage each person to engage fully in this journey—they will get out of it only as much as they invest. The purpose for the daily reinforcement activities is *not* to add busy work to their lives. This is actually a way to cultivate a habit of Bible study and daily time pursuing God's Presence, starting with just 15–20 minutes. Morning, evening, afternoon—*when* does not matter. The key is making the decision to engage.

OPENING PRAYER

WORSHIP (15 MINUTES—OPTIONAL FOR FIRST MEETING)

If a group chooses to do a worship segment, often they decide to begin on the second week. It usually takes an introductory meeting for everyone to become acquainted with one another and comfortable with their surroundings before they open up in worship.

On the other hand, if the group members are already comfortable with one another and they are ready to launch right into a time of worship, they should definitely go for it!

PRAYER/MINISTRY TIME (5–15 MINUTES)

VIDEO/TEACHING (20 MINUTES)

SCRIPTURE

*Now David was greatly distressed, for the people spoke of stoning him, because the soul of all the people was grieved, every man for his sons and his daughters. **But David strengthened himself in the Lord his God** (SAMUEL 30:6).*

SUMMARY

To fulfill your destiny in God, you need to learn the practical yet powerful steps to strengthening yourself in the Lord. This is how King David persevered through his long season of process. Even though David was anointed by the prophet Samuel and received a significant promise—to be king—ultimately, there was a great span of time between his promise received (at his anointing) and promised fulfilled (when he finally becomes king). Even though there were countless opportunities for David to give up, he persevered. When absolutely everyone turned against him, from mentor-turned-enemy King Saul to his previously devoted mighty men, he made a destiny-defining choice that ultimately positioned him to step into his greatest hour of promotion: David strengthened himself in the Lord.

During these eight powerful sessions, Pastor Bill Johnson will share keys from the life of David and from his own journey with God that will keep you spiritually strong through difficult times. The goal is not simply to strengthen yourself so that your circumstances can improve and you can step into divine promotion. That's step one. Your life of breakthrough is meant to change the world around you. God created you to be a divine change-agent in your sphere of influence. Get ready to discover practical secrets to release the strength, power, and joy of God's kingdom *in your life* and *to your world*.

DISCUSSION QUESTIONS (25–30 MINUTES)

1. There were many years between David's anointing (promise received) and David stepping into his destiny (promise fulfilled).

   Why do you think it's *very important* for there to be time in between promise received and promise fulfilled?

2. What does it mean that God cannot put something heavy on a weak foundation?

3. How does strengthening yourself in the Lord position you to fulfill your divine destiny and not give up during times of pressure?

4. In this study, we will address the topic of promotion frequently.

   Discuss what you think promotion means and explore why you think that, biblically, promotion is very important to God.

5. It is possible for your most significant breakthroughs and destiny-defining promotions to come during/after seasons of tremendous difficulty. (Consider the life of David.)

   To keep yourself strong, why do you think it's so important *not* to: 1) blame God when things don't work out the way you thought they would, or 2) move into shame or guilt, blaming yourself?

6. Based on 1 Kings 10:9 (the statement made about Solomon), what is the end result of personal promotion? Why do you think it's so important to maintain this perspective?

7. Have participants share personal stories (as they feel comfortable) of times in their lives when they experienced significant opposition and difficulty—where immediately after the difficulty, they entered into seasons of promotion and breakthrough. During these difficult times, how did they specifically:

   a. Strengthen themselves in the Lord

   b. Persevere

   c. Learn from their mistakes

   d. Arrive at promotion and breakthrough

ACTIVATION: LEARN TO RECOGNIZE YOUR AREA OF PROMOTION

All of us are being summoned into new areas of promotion, as God is all about taking us from *glory to glory*.

Today, you are going to learn how to identify these areas with greater clarity so you can more effectively cooperate with the Holy Spirit as He leads you into new places of advancement and breakthrough. (Take 15–20 minutes, as time permits.)

1. Pray and ask the Holy Spirit to show you what areas in your life He wants to promote. (It could be

anything from growing in your spiritual life, to advancing in your job, to improving a specific relationship, to fulfilling a dream or desire you have, to following through on a career ambition.) *There could be multiple areas.*

2. Don't overwhelm yourself if many areas of promotion come to your mind during this exercise. Focus on a select few—*one* is probably most advisable.

3. Ask the Lord, *What area do You want me to focus on in this next season?* Even though there might be a few, it's best to start somewhere. Most likely, the Lord will highlight something to you.

4   Write this area of promotion down. Commit to praying over it during the course of the eight-week curriculum (and beyond).

    Ask if there are group members who would like to share what the Holy Spirit said to them about new areas of promotion. Have 2-3 people share.

Goal: The goal of this exercise is to remove the barriers of what you think promotion means. It's not just about making more money or securing a new title at your job; at its core, promotion is about you stepping into the divine destiny that God has planned for you! The purpose of these sessions is to help you become a person who is fit for supernatural promotion.

This will only come as you learn how to strengthen yourself in the Lord!

PLANS FOR THE NEXT WEEK (2 MINUTES)

Point out Day 1 through Day 5 in the workbook. Encourage everyone to participate fully in this daily journey in order to get the most out of it.

CLOSE IN PRAYER

$\mathcal{W}eek$ 1

VIDEO LISTENING GUIDE

Two things that cripple the people of God:

1. <u>Bitterness</u> (or resentment).

2. <u>Disappointment</u>.

David functioned as a:

1. <u>King</u>.

2. <u>Priest</u>.

3. <u>Prophet</u>.

   Your <u>tests</u> prove the grace of God that is on your life.

   How to get positioned to minister strength to yourself: Become <u>un-offendable</u>.

Two areas to avoid in order to strengthen yourself in the Lord:

1. Don't <u>blame</u> God.

2. Don't move into shame or <u>guilt</u>.

The purpose of promotion:

1. God acknowledging the <u>grace</u> that's functioning in us.

2. God positions us in a place where the people around us will <u>benefit</u> from our promotion.

⎯⎯⎯⎯⎯⎯⎯⎯⎯⎯ ⟨⟩ ⎯⎯⎯⎯⎯⎯⎯⎯⎯⎯

DRAWING STRENGTH FROM GOD'S PROMISES

Prayer Focus: Ask the Lord to help every participant recognize promises they have received from God and renew their trust in the Lord to bring those promises to pass.

FELLOWSHIP AND WELCOME (15–20 MINUTES)

Welcome everyone as they walk in. Be sure to identify any new members who were not at the previous session, have them introduce themselves so everyone is acquainted, and be sure that they receive the appropriate materials—workbook and book.

In the small group, **serve refreshments and facilitate fellowship** between group members. In a class setting, talk with the attendees—ask how their week has been and maintain a focus on what God *has done* and *is doing*.

Encourage everyone to gather in the meeting place. If it is a classroom setting, make an announcement that it is time to sit down and begin the session. If it is a small group, ensure everyone makes their way to the designated meeting space.

OPENING PRAYER

WORSHIP (15–20 MINUTES)

When it comes to the worship element, it can be executed in both small group and church class settings. While a worship time is not mandatory, it is highly encouraged, as the fundamental goal of this curriculum is to foster each participant's increased understanding and outworking of the supernatural realm. This is where true, lasting transformation takes place. Worship is a wonderful way of opening each session and setting everyone's perspective on what the class is about—not accumulating more information, but pursuing the One who is at the center of it all.

PRAYER/MINISTRY TIME (5–15 MINUTES)

VIDEO/TEACHING (20 MINUTES)

SCRIPTURE

Jerusalem has sinned gravely, Therefore she has become vile. All who honored her despise her Because they have seen her nakedness; Yes, she sighs and turns away. Her uncleanness is in her skirts; She did not consider her destiny; Therefore her collapse was awesome (LAMENTATIONS 1:8-9).

SUMMARY

In the Book of Lamentations, the prophet Jeremiah provides readers with a startling example of what happens when we *do not live mindful of* God's promises for our lives. The problem for many believers is that they are not quite sure how to carry God's promises to the place of fulfillment. This is exactly what you will be exploring in this session—practical ways that you can draw spiritual strength from reviewing God's promises. Living mindful of these promises is essential nourishment for every believer because they serve constant notice that there is a great destiny awaiting us.

Consider it this way: Every prophetic promise is a snapshot of God's intended future reality for your life. How do you receive a promise? An omniscient God sees the future and sets a glimpse of that future before your *present*. This glimpse is designed to fuel strength and perseverance within you. Not only is a promise purposed to motivate you onward, empowering you to press past resistance and step into the future that God is inviting you into, promises keep you connected to your divine destiny in God and encourage you never to settle for anything that is beneath them. Israel did not stay mindful of her divine destiny, and as a result *her collapse was awesome.* The opposite is also true. As you *consider* your destiny in God—as revealed by the great and precious promises that He gives—you are compelled onward to fulfill your potential and walk out your purpose!

DISCUSSION QUESTIONS (25–30 MINUTES)

1. Consider Lamentations 1:8-9. Discuss why you think Israel fell because the people did not consider their destiny.

2. How do the promises of God keep you mindful of your destiny *in* God?

3. What is a promise of God? **Get some different answers and discuss.**

4. How do promises from God strengthen you to press onward toward fulfilling your destiny?

5. Review and discuss some of the ways that you can draw strength from God's promises. **Encourage group members to share examples of how they might have put these principles to work in their lives.**

6. What is your "history with God," and how can reminding yourself of this history keep you strengthened to keep standing on God's promises (even in the midst of difficulty, resistance, and circumstances)?

7. What promises have you received from God that have come to pass (that have pushed you toward fulfilling your destiny, calling, and purpose)? **Ask for a few people to share.**

After people share their stories of promises fulfilled, transition immediately to the *Activation Exercise*. The goal of having people share testimonies of promises that have come to pass is to strengthen faith to engage the activation exercise.

ACTIVATION: IDENTIFYING PROMISES THAT NEED TO BE CULTIVATED AND STRENGTHENED

In the same way that you have seen God fulfill promises in your life, there are most likely promises that have *not* yet come to pass. Today, you will identify what some of these promises are and approach them with fresh faith.

1.   Ask group/class to break up into individuals (this will be more of an individualized activation exercise).

2.   Encourage everyone to have some kind of writing tool ready (paper, tablet, smartphone, etc.). They can also choose to write in their *Strengthen Yourself in the Lord* study guides.

3.   Have everyone spend some time in prayer and reflection (5–15 minutes, however long seems appropriate), and encourage participants to meditate on promises that the Lord has given them.

Maybe it's a promise concerning a specific circumstance, breakthrough, miracle, an impossible situation, a future calling, etc.

These promises also might have come in the form of prophetic words that were released over their lives.

4. Write down the promise(s). You can use the space below:

_____

_____

_____

_____

_____

_____

_____

_____

_____

_____

_____

_____

_____

_____

_____

_____

_____

_____

_____

Give participants the opportunity to share their promises, if they feel comfortable doing so.

Encourage participants to keep these promises in front of them _regularly_ throughout the week—and throughout their lives!

Goal: To train participants to record promises of God and keep these promises in front of themselves constantly. Promises are God's way of keeping His people mindful of their destiny in Him.

PLANS FOR THE NEXT WEEK (2 MINUTES)

Encourage group members to stay up to date with their daily exercises in the _Strengthen Yourself in the Lord Workbook_.

CLOSE IN PRAYER

VIDEO LISTENING GUIDE

To strengthen ourselves in the Lord, we must stay connected to the <u>promises</u> of God.

God gives us promises to draw and invite us into our <u>future</u>.

How to Draw Strength from God's Promises

1. We are called to prayerfully <u>meditate</u> on God's promises—not make them happen by ourselves.

2. Let God's promises shape us so that we become people who <u>anticipate</u> the fulfillment of what God has declared over our lives.

3. Keep the truth of God's <u>goodness</u> as the cornerstone of theology.

4. Don't allow what you don't understand to <u>dislodge</u> what you do understand.

5. Avoid the traps of: 1) <u>blaming</u> God and 2) falling into guilt and shame.

6. Maintain your position of trust in the <u>character</u> of God and the promise of God in the middle of not having your answer or the needed breakthrough.

7. Draw strength from your personal <u>history</u> with God.

The safest place for the believer is on the <u>front lines</u> of battle.

THE SUPERNATURAL POWER OF THANKSGIVING

Prayer Focus: Ask the Lord to help every participant grow in having a thankful heart no matter what situation they are in.

FELLOWSHIP AND WELCOME (10–15 MINUTES)

Welcome everyone as they walk in. Be sure to identify any new members who were not at the previous session, and be sure that they receive the appropriate materials—workbook and book.

Encourage everyone to congregate in the meeting place. If it is a classroom setting, make an announcement that it is time to sit down and begin the session. If it is a small group, ensure everyone makes their way to the designated meeting space.

OPENING PRAYER

WORSHIP (15–20 MINUTES)

PRAYER/MINISTRY TIME (5–15 MINUTES)

VIDEO/TEACHING (20 MINUTES)

SCRIPTURE

Enter into His gates with thanksgiving (PSALM 100:4).

SUMMARY

Thanksgiving is absolutely vital to entering the gates of the Lord and receiving supernatural strength from His Presence. In fact, it is very difficult for us to move into the place of genuine praise apart from thanksgiving. While praise responds to the nature of God, thanksgiving celebrates the acts of God. Thanksgiving is intentional about parading before our minds the mighty acts, works, and miraculous exploits of the Lord—and responds to them with enthusiasm and gratitude. Thanksgiving is a strong and steady anchor for our hearts, as it keeps us ever mindful of what God *is doing* rather than buying into the lack-based perspective of an enemy who is always trying to get the people of God focused on what is supposedly *not* happening.

We strengthen ourselves in the Lord by choosing an attitude of thanksgiving, as this helps us to stay more aware of what God *is doing*, how God *is moving*, and what God *is bringing to pass* in our lives, rather than crumbling before the circumstances or impossibilities that seek to intimidate us.

DISCUSSION QUESTIONS (25-30 MINUTES)

1. How does thanksgiving keep us in a place of humility?

2. Explain how thanksgiving is part of the protocol for entering God's Presence. (Psalm 100:4—the relationship between thanksgiving and praise.)

3. Describe how living in a place of thanksgiving keeps you *more* mindful of God's work in your life.

4. Based on 1 Timothy 4:1-5, how can thanksgiving sanctify and cleanse?

5. Discuss some of the different benefits of thanksgiving. **Have participants share testimonies of how staying thankful—even during difficult times—kept their hearts strong.**

6. What does it mean to offer up thanks, even in times of mystery?

7. What does the following statement mean to you: "Faith does not deny a problem's existence; it denies it the place of influence."

8. In this session, Pastor Bill taught about how thanksgiving disarms the devil and puts his weapon into *your hand*. **Invite participants to share testimonies of how thanksgiving actually turned their circumstance around.**

ACTIVATION: RECALIBRATE YOUR HEART WITH THANKSGIVING

This will be a *group exercise.*

If possible, have praise and worship music ready to go—either live, or on some kind of audio system.

First, encourage participants to identify the following: 1) what they are thankful for, and 2) what they are thankful in the *midst of.*

During this time, encourage participants to make a list of things they are thankful for. (Approximately 10 minutes.)

Also, encourage them to honestly list out the circumstances or situations they are presently dealing with—that they will choose to be thankful *in the midst of.*

Reminder: this is *not* encouraging the participants to be thankful *for* their circumstances or claim that God sent these difficulties their way. Instead, thanksgiving is a supernatural act that causes them to: 1) lift their eyes to God, 2) acknowledge the circumstance in its proper place—subservient to God, and 3) specifically recognize the good things that God has done in their lives.

Second, after these things are identified and written down, have a time of praise and worship. This is a time to expressively offer up thanksgiving to God, and in the process of doing so disarm the powers of the enemy.

Goal: Learn to become more aware of what God has done and is doing in your life than the circumstances you are going through.

PLANS FOR THE NEXT WEEK (2 MINUTES)

Encourage group members to stay up to date with their daily exercises in the *Strengthen Yourself in the Lord Workbook.*

CLOSE IN PRAYER

Week 3

VIDEO LISTENING GUIDE

Any area of our lives where we have no <u>hope</u> is under the influence of lie.

Benefits of Thanksgiving

1. Thanksgiving keeps you in a place of <u>humility</u>.

2. Thanksgiving keeps you in the <u>center</u> of what God is doing.

3. Thanksgiving enables you to stay <u>aware</u> of God, His Presence, and His promise.

4. Thanksgiving gives you an <u>audience</u> with the King.

    In thanksgiving and praise, what we <u>say</u> is the offering.

    In worship, we <u>are</u> the offering.

5. Thanksgiving can supernaturally change our <u>circumstances</u>.

6. Thanksgiving <u>sanctifies</u>.

7.   Thanksgiving continues, even when there is
     <u>mystery</u>.

     Whenever there is death, loss, and destruction,
     you've seen the fingerprints of the <u>devil</u>.

     Faith does not deny a problem's existence; it denies
     it a place of <u>influence</u>.

PRAISE THAT RELEASES STRENGTH

Prayer Focus: Ask the Holy Spirit to give each participant ideas on how they can most effectively and biblically offer up praise—particularly in the midst of difficult situations, even if they don't feel like praising God.

FELLOWSHIP AND WELCOME (10–15 MINUTES)

Welcome everyone as they walk in. Be sure to identify any new members who were not at the previous session, and be sure that they receive the appropriate materials—workbook and book.

Encourage everyone to congregate in the meeting place. If it is a classroom setting, make an announcement that it is time to sit down and begin the session. If it is a small group, ensure everyone makes their way to the designated meeting space.

OPENING PRAYER

WORSHIP (15–20 MINUTES)

PRAYER/MINISTRY TIME (5–15 MINUTES)

VIDEO/TEACHING (25 MINUTES)

SCRIPTURE

Enter into His gates with thanksgiving, And into His courts with praise (PSALM 100:4).

He made known His ways to Moses, His acts to the children of Israel (PSALM 103:7).

SUMMARY

It is possible for people to offer thanksgiving to God without praising Him. This is when we simply give thanks for what God has done, but don't see past the breakthrough and actually become acquainted with the *Lord of the breakthrough*. Even those who don't know God are able to recognize the unusual blessing or favor of the Lord at work.

Thanksgiving naturally leads into praise. While thanksgiving applauds the works of God—just as the people of Israel did—praise goes deeper and searches out the ways of God's heart. Israel chose to stand at a distance while Moses went up into the cloud of Presence at Mt. Sinai. Even though his journey into the darkness could have been costly, he was simply not content sitting at the base of the mountain, simply observing the acts of God as a spectator, when in fact the invitation was extended for Moses to experientially know the very character of God. Praise sees God's nature in every act that He performs and responds accordingly!

DISCUSSION QUESTIONS (25–30 MINUTES)

1. How do thanksgiving and praise work together? (Review Psalm 100:4.)

2. Describe how the acts of God reveal His nature and ways.

3. What are some of the different ways that praise strengthens you in the Lord? **Ask some group members to share about times in their lives when their praise was directly connected to receiving supernatural strength.**

4. What is the difference between knowing the acts of God (like the children of Israel did) and knowing the ways of God (like Moses)? See Psalm 103:7.

5. How is it possible to give thanksgiving to God for one of His acts and still live at a distance from Him?

6. Based on Pastor Bill's testimony, how does the size of your circumstance determine the level of your praise? Why do you think it's important to offer up praise that responds to the size of your circumstance or difficulty?

7. **Encourage the group to share stories of how praise specifically brought them out of discouragement, sadness, depression, etc.**

This last question will transition immediately into the activation exercise.

ACTIVATION: LEARN HOW TO RECOGNIZE GOD'S NATURE IN HIS ACTS

Thanksgiving responds to the acts of God, while praise responds to His very nature. Today, you will have the opportunity to consider different things that you are thankful for and actually discover the DNA of God's nature in those mighty acts.

Directions: This can be an individual exercise, or the group/class can break up into smaller groups (two or three people).

1. Consider different works and acts of God that you have seen Him do in your life. (Start with some of the most recent and memorable.)

2. Write down these different works of God (5–8 minutes).

3. Discuss these with your small group. Share your testimony stories (1-2 stories per person depending on time), and then ask each other about what characteristics of God these different acts reveal.

4. Compile your lists.

5. At the end, have one person per group share to the larger group/class one act of God and what that act reveals about His nature.

6. As each act reveals a different facet and attribute of God's nature, praise builds up.

7. **If there is time at the end, we recommend having praise and worship.**

Goal: Your objective is to learn how to see the nature and character of God revealed in His acts.

PLANS FOR THE NEXT WEEK (2 MINUTES)

Encourage group members to stay up to date with their daily exercises in the *Strengthen Yourself in the Lord Workbook.*

CLOSE IN PRAYER

$\mathcal{W}eek$ 4

VIDEO LISTENING GUIDE

Personal breakthrough is intended to set us up for <u>corporate</u> breakthrough.

The presence of the Lord doesn't rest upon ministries; it rests upon <u>ministers</u>.

How does praise strengthen you in the Lord?

1.   Praise destroys <u>barrenness</u> and releases supernatural increase.

2.   Praise gives an <u>opposite</u> offering to what we think or feel in the midst of barren times.

3.   Praise <u>disarms</u> the enemy.

4.   Praise puts us in a <u>secure</u> place of triumph and victory.

5.   Praise demonstrates our <u>trustworthiness</u> for the breakthrough that we cry out for.

Any time we review the events of our past—apart from the blood of Jesus—we are visiting a <u>lie</u>.

Week 5

———— ⌒ ————

PRAYING WITH AUTHORITY, IDENTITY, AND INTIMACY

Prayer Focus: Ask the Holy Spirit to increase the ability of each participant to pray effectively—knowing when to rest in identity or demonstrate faith in authority.

FELLOWSHIP AND WELCOME (10–15 MINUTES)

Welcome everyone as they walk in. Be sure to identify any new members who were not at the previous session, and be sure that they receive the appropriate materials—workbook and book.

Encourage everyone to congregate in the meeting place. If it is a classroom setting, make an announcement that it is time to sit down and begin the session. If it is a small group, ensure everyone makes their way to the designated meeting space.

OPENING PRAYER

WORSHIP (15–20 MINUTES)

PRAYER/MINISTRY TIME (5–15 MINUTES)

Video/Teaching (20 minutes)

Scripture

And from the days of John the Baptist until now the kingdom of heaven suffers violence, and the violent take it by force (Matthew 11:12).

Assuredly, I say to you, whoever does not receive the kingdom of God as a little child will by no means enter it (Mark 10:15).

Summary

Prayer is the process through which we discover the character of God and, likewise, obtain the promises of God. It is not simply coming before God, presenting a list of prayer requests, and expecting Him to meet these needs. While He is more than happy to meet our needs, He is also inviting us into a deeper place of communion, intimacy, and fellowship. As we get to know God's nature and learn the ways of the Holy Spirit, we start to pick up on different approaches He might lead us to take in the place of prayer. We cannot afford to diminish a lifestyle of prayer to something that is purely transactional: "I prayed...now, God must deliver on my request."

In this session, you will learn how to recognize what prayer-approach to take in different situations and seasons of life. Our most important pursuit should be learning the ways of the Holy Spirit—which often comes by praying in the Spirit. This increases our awareness of what approach to prayer our situation needs. Remember, prayer is not a one-size-fits-all. There is a time for the violent demonstration of faith where we seize solutions in the invisible realm and forcefully release them into the visible (see Matt. 11:12). However, there is also a time for us to stand still and see the salvation of the Lord by simply receiving the Kingdom as little children (see 2 Chron. 20:17; Mark 10:15).

DISCUSSION QUESTIONS (25–30 MINUTES)

1. Describe the difference between the violence of faith (Matthew 11:12) and receiving the Kingdom as a child (Mark 10:15).

2. **Ask group members to share testimonies of both approaches to prayer. Specifically, ask if there is anyone who tried one approach and saw no results, only to try the other approach and experience breakthrough.**

3. What is the difference between God doing something *for* us and doing something *through us?*

4. How does knowing our authority in Christ empower us to become the kind of people God can work *through?*

5. What does Pastor Bill's statement mean to you: "If you're not hearing from God, talk to Him about

something He likes to talk about." Have you experienced seasons where you thought that you were not "hearing" from God? How did you change the conversation topic and start hearing His voice again?

6. Based on what Pastor Bill shared in this session, describe what the phrase *praying in the Holy Spirit* means. **Go around the group and ask for some different perspectives.**

7. How did your understanding of *praying in the Spirit* grow because of what you learned in this session? What benefits of praying in the Spirit have you personally experienced?

ACTIVATION: PRAYING ANOINTED PRAYERS

Break up into small groups (2-3 people) and pray for one another.

1. Share prayer needs with each other.

2. Ask the Holy Spirit to come and direct your time of prayer.

3. Pray for each other, one person at a time.

4. As you are praying, pay close attention to how the Holy Spirit leads and empowers your prayers.

5. After you pray, write down and document the moments where you sensed the Spirit moving

powerfully upon what you were praying (or what was being prayed over you).

Goal: Recognize the presence and power of the Spirit as you are praying for each other. This exercise is designed to increase your confidence in flowing with movement of the Holy Spirit in your prayers, for it is the Spirit who supernaturally strengthens our prayers and causes them to produce results.

PLANS FOR THE NEXT WEEK (2 MINUTES)

Encourage group members to stay up to date with their daily exercises in the *Strengthen Yourself in the Lord Workbook*.

CLOSE IN PRAYER

Week 5

VIDEO LISTENING GUIDE

Faith <u>attracts</u> promises from God.

Two Keys that Bring Kingdom Advancement

1.   The <u>violence</u> of faith.

2.   Receiving the Kingdom as a <u>child</u>.

   Sometimes God would rather do something <u>through</u> us than something for us.

   The child who receives the Kingdom is learning about inheritance and <u>identity</u>.

Benefits of Praying in the Holy Spirit

1.   By praying in the Spirit, we <u>edify</u> ourselves (see 1 Cor. 14:4).

2.   By praying in the Spirit, we are praying the <u>will</u> of God—precisely (see Rom. 8:26-27).

3.   By praying in the Spirit, we discover the ways and the spontaneous <u>movement</u> of the Holy Spirit.

4. By praying in the Spirit, we are praying prayers that carry the same weight as <u>prophetic</u> words.

5. By praying in the Spirit, our minds become increasingly <u>renewed</u> to how God thinks about different situations.

   We either live by <u>fear</u> or love.

Week 6

KEEPING THE TESTIMONY

Prayer Focus: Ask the Lord to help every participant identify and remember testimonies of God's power in their lives so they can build up their own faith and release faith to others.

FELLOWSHIP AND WELCOME (10–15 MINUTES)

Welcome everyone as they walk in. Be sure to identify any new members who were not at the previous session, and be sure that they receive the appropriate materials—workbook and book.

Encourage everyone to congregate in the meeting place. If it is a classroom setting, make an announcement that it is time to sit down and begin the session. If it is a small group, ensure everyone makes their way to the designated meeting space.

OPENING PRAYER

WORSHIP (10–15 MINUTES)

PRAYER/MINISTRY TIME (5–15 MINUTES)

Video/Teaching (20 minutes)

Scripture

You shall diligently keep the commandments of the Lord your God, His testimonies, and His statutes which He has commanded you (Deuteronomy 6:17).

For the testimony of Jesus is the spirit of prophecy (Revelation 19:10).

Summary

In the same way that we are instructed to keep the commandments of the Lord, we have been summoned to also keep His testimonies. These stories of God's supernatural interventions in our lives must be precious. We should hold them close to us, as they are vital landmarks in our spiritual histories. When we come against new impossibilities—in our lives or in the lives of others—we have a history of reference points. Testimonies remind us of what God *did,* and based on the truth that He is no respecter of persons and that Jesus is the same yesterday, today and forever, we can expect that the God who did the impossible in the past *will* also do the impossible in the present.

Revelation 19:10 reminds us that our testimonies actually release supernatural, prophetic power as we share them. Every time we tell stories of the miracles that Jesus performed in our lives, we are prophesying that the God who moved *then* can *move again*. The goal of this session is to show how staying connected to past testimonies of God's miracle-working power gives us strength to confidently face the circumstances and impossibilities of today.

DISCUSSION QUESTIONS (25–30 MINUTES)

1. How does the Bible tell us to "keep the testimonies"? ✖

2. Why do you think it's so important for us to keep talking about the testimonies of what God has done? ✖

3. What are some dangers of *not* keeping the testimony? ✖

4. Explain how the following two Scriptures are essential when it comes to understanding and releasing the power of testimony:

   *Then Peter opened his mouth, and said, Of a truth I perceive that **God is no respecter of persons*** (ACTS 10:34 KJV). ✖

   Jesus Christ is the same yesterday, today, and forever (HEBREWS 13:8). ✖

5. How do testimonies define the lens through which we see our present circumstances?

6. Explain how testimonies can carry and release pro-phetic power. ✳

7. Discuss how testimonies reveal the nature and character of God. **Ask group members to share different testimonies of God's miraculous power in their lives. After sharing their story, discuss what aspect of God's nature that story reveals.**

ACTIVATION: SHARE TESTIMONIES AND RELEASE SUPERNATURAL STRENGTH

1. Individually, take time to *write down some of the mir-acles that God has done in your life.* Try to start with the most recent testimony, but if you have difficulty remembering any, start back with the last miracu-lous thing you saw God do in your life (or someone else's life).

2. Pick one specific testimony and share it before the group/class. (**Have as many group members do this as time allows**.)

3. After you share the testimony, ask if there is anyone in the group/class who is going through something similar to what God miraculously brought you out of.

   a. Invite these people to either: 1) come forward to receive prayer, or 2) stay where they are seated and have people next to them lay hands on them.

b. *Pray for these people and their needs out of your testimony.* In other words, because of what you have seen God do in your life, you are able to pray for these needs with fresh confidence and expectation of breakthrough.

c. Encourage the people you pray for to *share their breakthroughs* as they receive them. This is truly an example of keeping the testimony!

4. The next person will come up and share his/her testimony, repeating the process.

PLANS FOR THE NEXT WEEK (2 MINUTES)

Encourage group members to stay up to date with their daily exercises in the *Strengthen Yourself in the Lord Workbook.*

CLOSE IN PRAYER

VIDEO LISTENING GUIDE

Communicating the testimony should be a way of <u>life</u>.

The Testimony is:

1. Our <u>history</u> with God.

2. Our <u>inheritance</u>.

3. The written or spoken <u>record</u> of anything that God has done.

4. A revelation of God's <u>nature</u>.

5. The <u>lens</u> through which we see our present circumstance.

6. The spirit of <u>prophecy</u> that releases God's power to change present situations.

   Faith is <u>superior</u> reasoning.

THE IMPORTANCE OF CONTROLLING YOUR ENVIRONMENT

Prayer Focus: Ask the Lord to help every participant carefully monitor their personal lives, giving them wisdom to know what associations and practices are appropriate in each season.

FELLOWSHIP AND WELCOME (10–15 MINUTES)

Welcome everyone as they walk in. Be sure to identify any new members who were not at the previous session, and be sure that they receive the appropriate materials—workbook and book.

Encourage everyone to congregate in the meeting place. If it is a classroom setting, make an announcement that it is time to sit down and begin the session. If it is a small group, ensure everyone makes their way to the designated meeting space.

OPENING PRAYER

WORSHIP (15–20 MINUTES)

Feel free to shorten the worship time at the beginning of the session, as the activation exercise will consist of a worship segment.

PRAYER/MINISTRY TIME (5–15 MINUTES)

VIDEO/TEACHING (20 MINUTES)

SCRIPTURE

Then He said to them, "Take heed what you hear. With the same measure you use, it will be measured to you; and to you who hear, more will be given" (MARK 4:24).

SUMMARY

Jesus' cautionary statement in Mark 4 reminds us that *how* we hear is very important. We determine *how* we hear from people, media, and other avenues by intentionally controlling our environment. If we are going through difficult circumstances or we are in the middle of very fragile personal struggles, there is wisdom that we need to use when considering the messages (and messengers) that we are exposing ourselves to. The very things that may not impact us at all in one season could be life-draining and strength-depleting in another. This is why it is so important for us to control our environments—it is absolutely fundamental to strengthening ourselves in the Lord!

In this session, Pastor Bill offers some very practical advice on how we should control what/who we are exposed to. This is not a call to separatism—isolating ourselves from everyone else and becoming spiritual islands. The world needs the Kingdom solutions we carry. Rather, this is an invitation to wisdom. In the journey of life, there will be seasons where we cannot *closely* associate with certain people, or watch certain media, or be in certain places, or expose ourselves to certain atmospheres. In order to supernaturally change the atmosphere around us, it is essential to pay close attention to the unique seasons where we need to especially guard our personal environment. Our measure of Kingdom effectiveness *to the world* has everything to do with how we steward our private, interior lives.

DISCUSSION QUESTIONS (25–30 MINUTES)

1. Why it is important *how* we hear? Describe the difference between *what* you hear and *how* you hear.

2. Describe why it's important to discern what is acceptable for one season and what is not acceptable for another (certain associations with people, TV shows, places, media, etc.). **Ask some participants to share testimonies of how they took certain seasons of life and restricted certain interactions. Have them explain why this was beneficial to them.**

3. How can your environment/atmosphere impact your strength?

4. Why is it so important to discern what company/close fellowship you should keep with certain people?

5. How do people attract people of like values? Discuss how this can work for the positive and the negative.

6. Why it is so important about who you choose to *closely* share your life with?

7. Discuss how fellowship brings strength to our lives. **Have participants share testimonies of how their fellowship with others was actually key to bringing them into breakthrough/a place of strength.**

Activation: Evaluate Your Environment

This is an exercise for each participant to engage *individually*.

1. Prayerfully consider your current season of life. What are some specific areas you need strength in?

2. Ask the Holy Spirit to reveal areas that He wants to adjust. Specifically, ask Him about *people, places, media,* and other *activities* you are presently involved with that might need to be limited/restricted in this season...*for your benefit!*

You can write these out in the space below:

_____

_____

_____

_____

_____

_____

_____

_____

_____

_____

_____

_____

_____

Note: Remember, anything the Lord reveals to you is not for the purpose of condemnation; if there is something God wants you to *control* in your environment, it is for the purpose of bringing you into a greater place of strength and effectiveness.

PLANS FOR THE NEXT WEEK (2 MINUTES)

Encourage group members to stay up to date with their daily exercises in the *Strengthen Yourself in the Lord Workbook*.

CLOSE IN PRAYER

VIDEO LISTENING GUIDE

It's not unbelief to recognize a <u>fragile</u> season; it's wisdom.

Values <u>attract</u> like values—good or bad.

Steps to Controlling Your Environment

1. Evaluate what <u>contributes</u> to your life.

2. Be careful of the <u>standard</u> of what you are willing to entertain and listen to.

3. Carefully <u>select</u> who you are willing to closely share your life with.

4. Recognize seasons in your life when it's wisdom to <u>restrict</u> certain activities and associations.

5. Fellowship is a source of <u>strength</u>.

6. Fellowship is the <u>exchange</u> of life.

Week 8

THE PROCESS OF SUSTAINING A BREAKTHROUGH LIFESTYLE

Prayer Focus: Ask the Lord to give every participant a revelation of His unchanging goodness and faithfulness in the midst of challenging times, so that they can transition from being those who receive breakthrough to being people who release breakthrough to others.

FELLOWSHIP AND WELCOME (10–15 MINUTES)

Welcome everyone as they walk in. Be sure to identify any new members who were not at the previous session, and be sure that they receive the appropriate materials—workbook and book.

Encourage everyone to congregate in the meeting place. If it is a classroom setting, make an announcement that it is time to sit down and begin the session. If it is a small group, ensure everyone makes their way to the designated meeting space.

OPENING PRAYER

WORSHIP (15–20 MINUTES)

PRAYER/MINISTRY TIME (10 MINUTES)

VIDEO/TEACHING (20 MINUTES)

SCRIPTURE

Behaving as do those who through faith (by their leaning of the entire personality on God in Christ in absolute trust and confidence in His power, wisdom, and goodness) and by practice of patient endurance and waiting are [now] inheriting the promises (HEBREWS 6:12 AMP).

SUMMARY

In this session, Pastor Bill shares some practical insights that he has gleaned over the years on how to navigate through discouragement, remain anchored in God's goodness, and celebrate the amazing grace of Jesus in our lives—even before we see significant transformation take place! You will learn how the *process* to sustaining a breakthrough lifestyle has everything to do with protecting our hearts. There are many Christians who never sustain the supernatural life Jesus made available because they allow themselves to be derailed by a number of different factors—discouragement, disappointment, lack of instant results, perfectionism, etc. They may even be people who have experienced a miracle, received a healing, or prayed at one point and seen results. While scattered reports of miracles are worth celebrating, Jesus purchased so much more for

His people. Jesus didn't simply say that we would *see* or be spectators of the miraculous; He promised that "*he who believes in Me, the works that I do he will do also*" (John 14:12).

Who are the people fit to *do* the works of Jesus as a lifestyle? Not the perfect, the exclusive, or the super spiritual. Rather, the sustained miracle lifestyle of Jesus is reserved for those who place a high value on protecting their interior lives from contamination. What you will learn in this session and the accompanying exercises will help you guard your heart and show you how to be a good steward of what the Lord has deposited into your life. Kingdom promotion is the result of good stewardship. For those who use what they have *well*, they will be rewarded with increase. However, if we allow distraction, disappointment, discouragement, or anything else to get us off course, preventing us from walking in the measure of anointing and power we have received in the Holy Spirit, we will not experience increase.

There is more of God's power available than what we are presently witnessing and walking in. It's not God's sovereign will that is preventing us from walking in a greater demonstration of the supernatural; it is successfully navigating through these matters of the heart. By doing so, we are actually building up an interior life that the Spirit of God can rest upon in greater measure than ever before and use us to be agents of Kingdom breakthrough wherever the Lord has uniquely positioned us!

DISCUSSION QUESTIONS (25–30 MINUTES)

1. How can we let our circumstances and disappointments create a *healthy* anguish of soul (like Hannah and her desire for a child) that causes us to press in for breakthrough?

2. Describe how we can let problems actually drive us *into* God's Presence instead of leading us from Him. **Ask participants to share testimonies of how they may have let their circumstances drive them deeper into God's Presence.**

3. What do you think happens when we let our pain and disappointment keep us *away* from God's Presence? How does this impact the possibility of us sustaining breakthrough lifestyles?

4. Discuss the *process* of sustaining a breakthrough lifestyle. Compare/contrast the *process* with the desire to receive an instant, immediate miracle. How are the two different and why do you think it is so important to pursue the process?

5. What are some issues in life that might cause people to give up on the miraculous and stop believing God for the impossible? **Discuss how we should respond to these.**

6. How have you witnessed miracles and breakthrough by going through a *process*? **Ask**

participants to share what their individual processes looked like.

7. Explain why stewardship is so important to seeing Kingdom promotion in your life. (Consider David's journey and how he was a good steward.)

8. **Have group members share testimonies of how perseverance brought miracles and breakthroughs in their lives (instead of an instant miracle).**

ACTIVATION: PRESSING IN FOR MORE

1. Break up into small groups of 2-3 and pray for each other's needs.

2. Ask each other specifically about the needs/prayer requests that involve a *process* instead of an instant miracle or breakthrough.

3. Follow the Holy Spirit's guidance in prayer, releasing strength over each other to persevere and endure.

Once you are finished praying for each other in mini groups, come together as a complete group or class.

Take time to pray, corporately, for a greater anointing for perseverance, strength, and the ability to press on. This is key to spiritual maturity, particularly for those desiring to walk out the supernatural lifestyle.

PLANS FOR THE NEXT WEEK (2 MINUTES)

Let participants know that either this is the final week of the study or that you will be having some type of social activity on the following week—or at a specified future date.

CLOSE IN PRAYER

Pray that the group would truly be able to strengthen themselves in the Lord as they continue to daily walk out the tools that have been presented throughout the course.

$\mathcal{W}eek$ 8

VIDEO LISTENING GUIDE

We need to let problems drive us into the <u>presence</u> of God.

When we become fearful and anxious, we <u>forget</u> what God said.

Grace celebrates what we have <u>received</u> before we start acting differently.

The enemy wants to anchor your thought life in the <u>past</u> and what didn't work.

What you <u>celebrate</u> in is what you become.

The downfall of living in a miracle culture:

A people who avoid the <u>process</u> of growth and development because they prefer immediate, major breakthroughs.

Wilderness: Miracles <u>sustained</u> Israel.

Promise Land: Miracles <u>advanced</u> Israel.

God will invade where there is faithful <u>stewardship</u>.